SUPERHEROES ON A MEDICAL MISSION

MEDIKIDZ EXPLAIN SWINE FLU

rosen publishing's
rosen central

New York

Dr. Kim Chilman-Blair

Medical content reviewed for accuracy by Dr. John McCauley and Dr. Calum Semple

This edition published in 2011 by:

The Rosen Publishing Group, Inc.
29 East 21st Street
New York, NY 10010

Additional end matter copyright © 2011 by The Rosen Publishing Group, Inc.

Library of Congress Cataloging-in-Publication Data

Chilman-Blair, Kim.
 Medikidz explain swine flu / Kim Chilman-Blair ; medical content reviewed for accuracy by John McCauley and Calum Semple.
    p. cm. — (Superheroes on a medical mission)
 Includes bibliographical references and index.
 ISBN 978-1-4358-9457-0 (lib. bdg.) — ISBN 978-1-4488-1843-3 (pbk.) — ISBN 978-1-4488-1844-0 (6-pack)
 1. Swine influenza—Comic books, strips, etc—Juvenile literature. I. Title.
 RC150.C55 2011
 636.5'0896203—dc22
                              2010003236

Manufactured in China

CPSIA Compliance Information: Batch #MS0102YA: For further information, contact Rosen Publishing, New York, New York, at 1-800-237-9932.

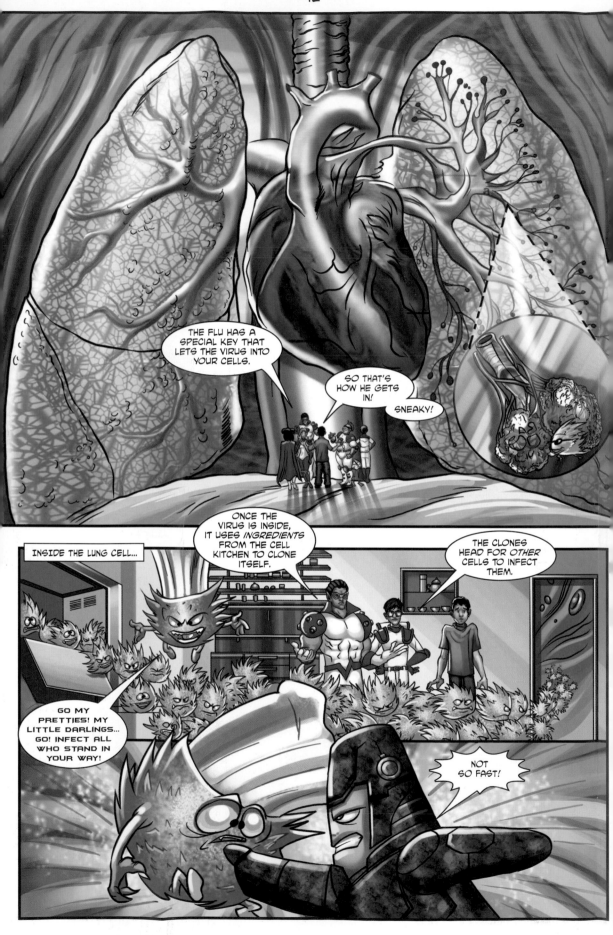

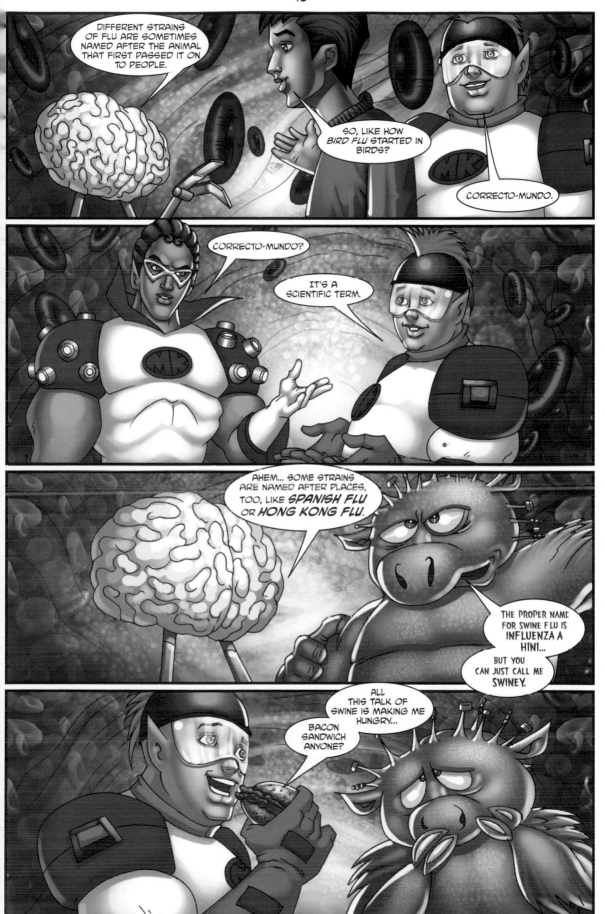

SO HOW DOES IT SPREAD?

THE VIRUS ESCAPES IN *WATER DROPLETS.*

THESE WATER DROPLETS GET INTO THE AIR WHEN PEOPLE *COUGH* OR *SNEEZE...*

...AND IF YOU *BREATHE* THEM IN, YOU CAN BECOME INFECTED.

THE VIRUS CAN TRAVEL ABOUT 3 FEET (1 METER) AFTER SOMEONE COUGHS OR SNEEZES.

THAT *MAN...* WHO SNEEZED ON JASMINE!

IF I EVER SEE HIM, I'M GOING TO TAMIFLU HIS FACE!

GUYS, I REALLY APPRECIATE EVERYTHING YOU'VE TAUGHT ME, BUT I THINK IT'S TIME I GOT BACK HOME SO I CAN TEACH JASMINE ALL ABOUT SWINE FLU, AND TO HELP HER GET BETTER!
MY BED IS CALLING ME, TOO. IT'S SHAPED LIKE A HAMBURGER, YOU KNOW. I GET TO BE THE MEAT!

GOOD-BYE MEDIKIDZ! THANKS FOR EVERYTHING!
GOOD-BYE VIJAY!
click!!!

ANTIBIOTICS CHEMICAL SUBSTANCES THAT CAN CURE
    INFECTIONS BY KILLING THE HARMFUL BACTERIA.

ANTIVIRAL EFFECTIVE AGAINST VIRUSES.

BACTERIA (SINGULAR, BACTERIUM) MICROSCOPIC SINGLE-
    CELL ORGANISMS, SOME OF WHICH CAN CAUSE
    DISEASES.

BIRD FLU ALSO KNOWN AS AVIAN FLU, A TYPE OF
    INFLUENZA THAT AFFECTS BIRDS, INCLUDING
    DOMESTIC CHICKENS, AND IS CAPABLE OF INFECTING
    HUMANS.

BLOODSTREAM THE FLOW OF BLOOD CIRCULATING IN THE
    BLOOD VESSELS OF A PERSON OR ANIMAL.

CHICKEN POX A HIGHLY INFECTIOUS VIRAL DISEASE,
    ESPECIALLY AFFECTING CHILDREN, CHARACTERIZED BY
    A RASH OF SMALL ITCHING BLISTERS ON THE SKIN
    AND A MILD FEVER.

CLONE A COLLECTION OF ORGANISMS OR CELLS THAT ARE
    GENETICALLY IDENTICAL.

COMMON COLD A VIRAL INFECTION OF THE NOSE
    AND THROAT, CHARACTERIZED BY SNEEZING, NASAL
    CONGESTION, COUGHING, AND HEADACHE.

DIARRHEA FREQUENT AND EXCESSIVE BOWEL
    MOVEMENTS, PRODUCING THIN WATERY DISCHARGE,
    USUALLY AS A SIGN OF UPSET OR AN INFECTION.

HONG KONG FLU A TYPE OF INFLUENZA CAUSED BY
    INFLUENZA A (H3N2) THAT WAS RESPONSIBLE FOR A
    PANDEMIC IN 1968-1969.

IMMUNE SYSTEM A SYSTEM THAT PROTECTS THE BODY
    AGAINST DISEASE.

INFECTION A DISEASE THAT IS CATCHING; AN INFECTING
    MICROORGANISM.

INFLUENZA ALSO CALLED FLU, A VIRAL ILLNESS THAT
    PRODUCES A HIGH TEMPERATURE, SORE THROAT,
    RUNNY NOSE, HEADACHE, DRY COUGH, AND MUSCLE
    PAIN.

INGREDIENTS ITEMS IN A RECIPE; COMPONENTS OF A
    MIXTURE.

INVADE TO ENTER OR SPREAD THROUGH SOMETHING.

MITOSIS CELL DIVISION; THE PROCESS BY WHICH A CELL
    DIVIDES INTO TWO DAUGHTER CELLS, EACH OF WHICH
    HAS THE SAME NUMBER OF CHROMOSOMES AS THE
    ORIGINAL CELL.

MUCUS A CLEAR, SLIMY LUBRICATING SUBSTANCE THAT

COATS AND PROTECTS MUCOUS MEMBRANES.

MUTATION A CHANGE IN GENETIC MATERIAL; THE ACTION OR PROCESS OF CHANGING SOMETHING OR OF BEING CHANGED.

PANDEMIC HAVING WIDESPREAD EFFECT, AS IN THE FORM OF A WIDESPREAD DISEASE OR CONDITION THAT AFFECTS PEOPLE IN MANY DIFFERENT COUNTRIES.

PARASITE AN ORGANISM THAT LIVES ON A HOST ORGANISM IN A WAY THAT HARMS THE HOST.

PNEUMONIA INFLAMMATION OF ONE OR BOTH LUNGS, USUALLY CAUSED BY AN INFECTION FROM A BACTERIUM OR VIRUS.

PRIME TO MAKE OR BECOME READY; TO MAKE SOMETHING READY FOR USE OR BECOME READY FOR USE.

SPANISH FLU A PANDEMIC OF INFLUENZA A (H1N1) IN 1918-1919 THAT CAUSED HUNDREDS OF THOUSANDS OF PEOPLE TO DIE IN THE UNITED STATES AND MILLIONS WORLDWIDE. ALMOST HALF OF THOSE WHO DIED WERE YOUNG ADULTS.

STRAINS SUBGROUPS OF A SPECIES OF ORGANISM THAT ARE DISTINGUISHED BY SPECIFIC CHARACTERISTICS.

SWINE FLU (INFLUENZA A H1N1) A TYPE OF INFLUENZA A (H1N1) THAT IS CAUSED BY A DIFFERENT STRAIN OF H1N1 FROM THOSE FOUND IN SWINE AND THAT IS MARKED BY FEVER, SORE THROAT, COUGH, CHILLS, BODY ACHES, FATIGUE, AND DIARRHEA AND VOMITING.

TAMIFLU A TRADEMARKED NAME FOR OSELTAMIVIR, AN ANTIVIRAL DRUG USED TO TREAT FLU, INCLUDING SWINE FLU.

VACCINE A MEDICATION GIVEN TO A HEALTHY PERSON FOR THE PURPOSE OF PREVENTING A SPECIFIC DISEASE.

VIRUS A TINY GERM THAT NEEDS TO ENTER THE CELLS OF A LIVING ORGANISM TO BECOME ACTIVATED AND MULTIPLY.

VOMIT TO THROW UP STOMACH CONTENTS THROUGH THE MOUTH AS A RESULT OF A SERIES OF INVOLUNTARY SPASMS OF THE STOMACH MUSCLES.

FOR MORE INFORMATION

CENTERS FOR DISEASE CONTROL AND PREVENTION (CDC)
U.S. DEPARTMENT OF HEALTH AND HUMAN SERVICES
1600 CLIFTON ROAD
ATLANTA, GA 30333
(404) 498-1515
WEB SITE: HTTP://WWW.CDC.GOV
THE CDC PROVIDES ONLINE INFORMATION ABOUT ALL TYPES OF
        DISEASES AND MEDICAL CONDITIONS.

HEALTH CANADA
BROOKE CLAXTON BUILDING, TUNNY'S PASTURE
POSTAL LOCATOR: 0906C
OTTAWA, ON K1A OK9
CANADA
WEB SITE: HTTP://WWW.HC-SC.GC.CA/INDEX-ENG.PHP
HEALTH CANADA IS CANADA'S FEDERAL DEPARTMENT
        RESPONSIBLE FOR HEALTH CONCERNS. SEE ESPECIALLY
        THE "INFLUENZA (FLU)" SECTION.

NATIONAL INSTITUTES OF HEALTH (NIH)
U.S. DEPARTMENT OF HEALTH AND HUMAN SERVICES
9000 ROCKVILLE PIKE
BETHESDA, MD 20892
(301) 496-4000
WEB SITE: HTTP://WWW.NIH.GOV
THE NIH IS THE PRIMARY U.S. GOVERNMENT AGENCY FOR
        CONDUCTING AND SUPPORTING MEDICAL RESEARCH.

NATIONAL LIBRARY OF MEDICINE
8600 ROCKVILLE PIKE
BETHESDA, MD 20894
(888) 346-3656
WEB SITE: HTTP://WWW.NLM.NIH.GOV
THIS HUGE BIOLOGICAL LIBRARY IS PART OF THE NIH. ITS
        MEDLINEPLUS WEB SITE PROVIDES THE CURRENT
        INFORMATION ABOUT SWINE FLU, MEDICATIONS, AND
        TREATMENTS.

PUBLIC HEALTH AGENCY OF CANADA
130 COLONNADE ROAD
A.L. 6501H
OTTAWA, ON K1A OK9
CANADA
WEB SITE: HTTP://WWW.PHAC-ASPC.GC.CA
THIS AGENCY'S MISSION IS "TO PROMOTE AND PROTECT THE
        HEALTH OF CANADIANS THROUGH LEADERSHIP,
        PARTNERSHIP, INNOVATION, AND ACTION IN PUBLIC HEALTH."

SEE THE "FIGHTFLU.CA" PAGE FOR INFORMATION ABOUT THE SWINE FLU.

U.S. DEPARTMENT OF HEALTH AND HUMAN SERVICES
200 INDEPENDENCE AVENUE SW
WASHINGTON, DC 20201
WEB SITE: HTTP://WWW.FLU.GOV
MANAGED BY THE U.S. DEPARTMENT OF HEALTH AND HUMAN
    SERVICES, THIS WEB SITE PROVIDES THE PUBLIC WITH
    INFORMATION REGARDING WHAT TO DO ABOUT SEASONAL,
    SWINE, BIRD, AND PANDEMIC FLU.

U.S. FOOD AND DRUG ADMINISTRATION (FDA)
U.S. DEPARTMENT OF HEALTH AND HUMAN SERVICES
5600 FISHERS LANE
ROCKVILLE, MD 20857-0001
(888) 463-6332
WEB SITE: HTTP://WWW.FDA.GOV
THE FDA PUBLISHES INFORMATION ON ALL FOOD AND
    DRUG REGULATION. SEE ESPECIALLY THE WEB SECTION
    FOR H1N1 (SWINE) FLU (HTTP://WWW.FDA.GOV/NEWSEVENTS/
    PUBLICHEATHFOCUS/UCM150305.HTM).

WORLD HEALTH ORGANIZATION (WHO)
AVENUE APPIA 20
1211 GENEVA 27
SWITZERLAND
+ 41 22 791 21 11
WEB SITE: HTTP://WWW.WHO.INT/CSR/DISEASE/SWINEFLU/EN/
WHO IS THE INTERNATIONAL AGENCY FOR HEALTH WITHIN THE
    UNITED NATIONS SYSTEM THAT IS RESPONSIBLE FOR
    DIRECTING GLOBAL HEALTH MATTERS AND TRACKING
    HEALTH TRENDS, INCLUDING INFLUENZA OUTBREAKS.

WEB SITES

DUE TO THE CHANGING NATURE OF INTERNET LINKS, ROSEN
PUBLISHING HAS DEVELOPED AN ONLINE LIST OF WEB SITES
RELATED TO THE SUBJECT OF THIS BOOK. THIS SITE IS UPDATED
REGULARLY. PLEASE USE THIS LINK TO ACCESS THIS LIST:

HTTP://WWW.ROSENLINKS.COM/MED/SWIN

DORRANCE, JOHN M., ED. *GLOBAL TIME BOMB: SURVIVING THE H1N1 SWINE FLU PANDEMIC AND OTHER GLOBAL HEALTH THREATS.* VANCOUVER ISLAND, BC: MADRONA BOOKS, 2009.

DUMAR, A. M. *SWINE FLU: WHAT YOU NEED TO KNOW.* BROOKLYN, NY: BROWNSTONE BOOKS, 2009.

EMMELUTH, DONALD. *INFLUENZA (DEADLY DISEASES AND EPIDEMICS).* 2ND ED. NEW YORK, NY: CHELSEA HOUSE PUBLISHERS, 2008.

GOLDSMITH, CONNIE. *INFLUENZA: THE NEXT PANDEMIC?* MINNEAPOLIS, MN: TWENTY-FIRST CENTURY BOOKS, 2007.

GRAY, SUSAN H. *DISEASE CONTROL* (INNOVATION IN MEDICINE). ANN ARBOR, MI: CHERRY LAKE PUBLISHING, 2009.

HARMON, DANIEL E. *NEW MEDICINES: ISSUES OF APPROVAL, ACCESS, AND PRODUCT SAFETY* (SCIENCE AND SOCIETY). NEW YORK, NY: ROSEN PUBLISHING GROUP, 2009.

KOHN, GEORGE CHILDS, ED. *ENCYCLOPEDIA OF PLAGUE AND PESTILENCE FROM ANCIENT TIMES TO THE PRESENT.* NEW YORK, NY: FACTS ON FILE, 2007.

KUPPERBERG, PAUL. *THE INFLUENZA PANDEMIC OF 1918-1919* (GREAT HISTORIC DISASTERS). NEW YORK, NY: CHELSEA HOUSE PUBLISHERS, 2008.

MASON, PAUL. *KNOW THE FACTS ABOUT PHYSICAL HEALTH* (KNOW THE FACTS). NEW YORK, NY: ROSEN PUBLISHING GROUP, 2010.

MAY, SUELLEN. *INVASIVE MICROBES* (INVASIVE SPECIES). NEW YORK, NY: CHELSEA HOUSE PUBLISHERS, 2007.

NAGLE, JEANNE. *FREQUENTLY ASKED QUESTIONS ABOUT AVIAN FLU* (FAQ: TEEN LIFE). NEW YORK, NY: ROSEN PUBLISHING GROUP, 2009.

ORR, TAMRA B. *AVIAN FLU* (COPING IN A CHANGING WORLD). NEW YORK, NY: ROSEN PUBLISHING GROUP, 2007.

SCIENTIFIC AMERICAN. *FIGHTING INFECTIOUS DISEASES* (SCIENTIFIC AMERICAN: CUTTING-EDGE SCIENCE). NEW YORK, NY: ROSEN PUBLISHING GROUP, 2007.

SEGALL, MIRIAM. *PANDEMICS* (IN THE NEWS). NEW YORK, NY: ROSEN PUBLISHING GROUP, 2007.

SIEGEL, MARC. *SWINE FLU: THE NEW PANDEMIC.* HOBOKEN, NJ: JOHN WILEY AND SONS, 2009.

SILVERSTEIN, LAURA, ALVIN SILVERSTEIN, AND VIRGINIA SILVERSTEIN. *THE FLU AND PNEUMONIA UPDATE* (DISEASE UPDATE). BERKELEY HEIGHTS, NJ: ENSLOW PUBLISHERS, 2006.

TURKINGTON, CAROL, AND BONNIE LEE ASHBY. *THE ENCYCLOPEDIA OF INFECTIOUS DISEASES.* 3RD ED. NEW YORK, NY: FACTS ON FILE, 2007.

WIWANITKIT, VIROJ. *SWINE FLU AND PIG BORNE DISEASES.* (PUBLIC HEALTH IN THE 21ST CENTURY). HAUPPAUGE, NY: NOVA SCIENCE PUBLISHERS, 2009.

ABOUT THE AUTHORS

DR. KIM CHILMAN-BLAIR IS A MEDICAL DOCTOR WITH TEN YEARS OF EXPERIENCE IN MEDICAL WRITING AND A PASSION FOR PROVIDING MEDICAL INFORMATION THAT MAKES CHILDREN WANT TO LEARN.